Some people have two Mums

For Steven and Riccardo - L.P.
For Lily and Atticus - F.K.

If you can, please buy two books - one for your child
and one to give away as a present or donation to a school
or library so together we can educate parents, children
and the community and make the world a better place.

www.Somefamilies.net

First published 2013

Text copyright © Fabri Kramer and Luca Panzini 2013
Illustrations copyright © Luca Panzini 2013
All rights reserved

ISBN: 1484097122   ISBN-13: 978-1484097120

Some people have two Mums

By Fabri Kramer and Luca Panzini

Illustrated by Luca Panzini

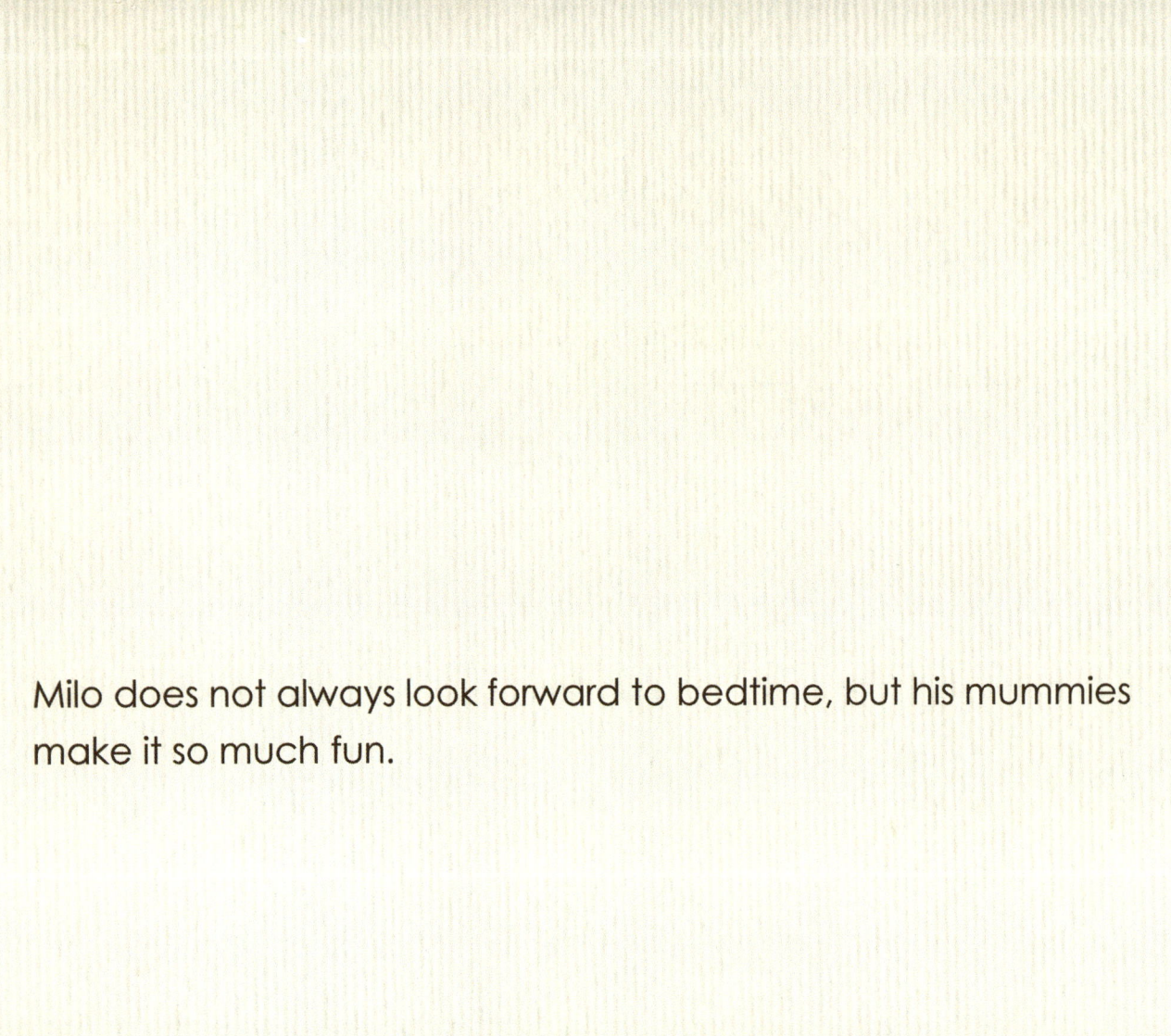

Milo does not always look forward to bedtime, but his mummies make it so much fun.

Tonight they are looking for Milo's favourite pajamas. Mummy thinks they are in the washing but Milo knows they were borrowed by an adventurer searching for dinosaurs.

At bathtime they help Milo battle against a giant octopus.
A cheeky shark splashes Mummy which makes them all laugh.

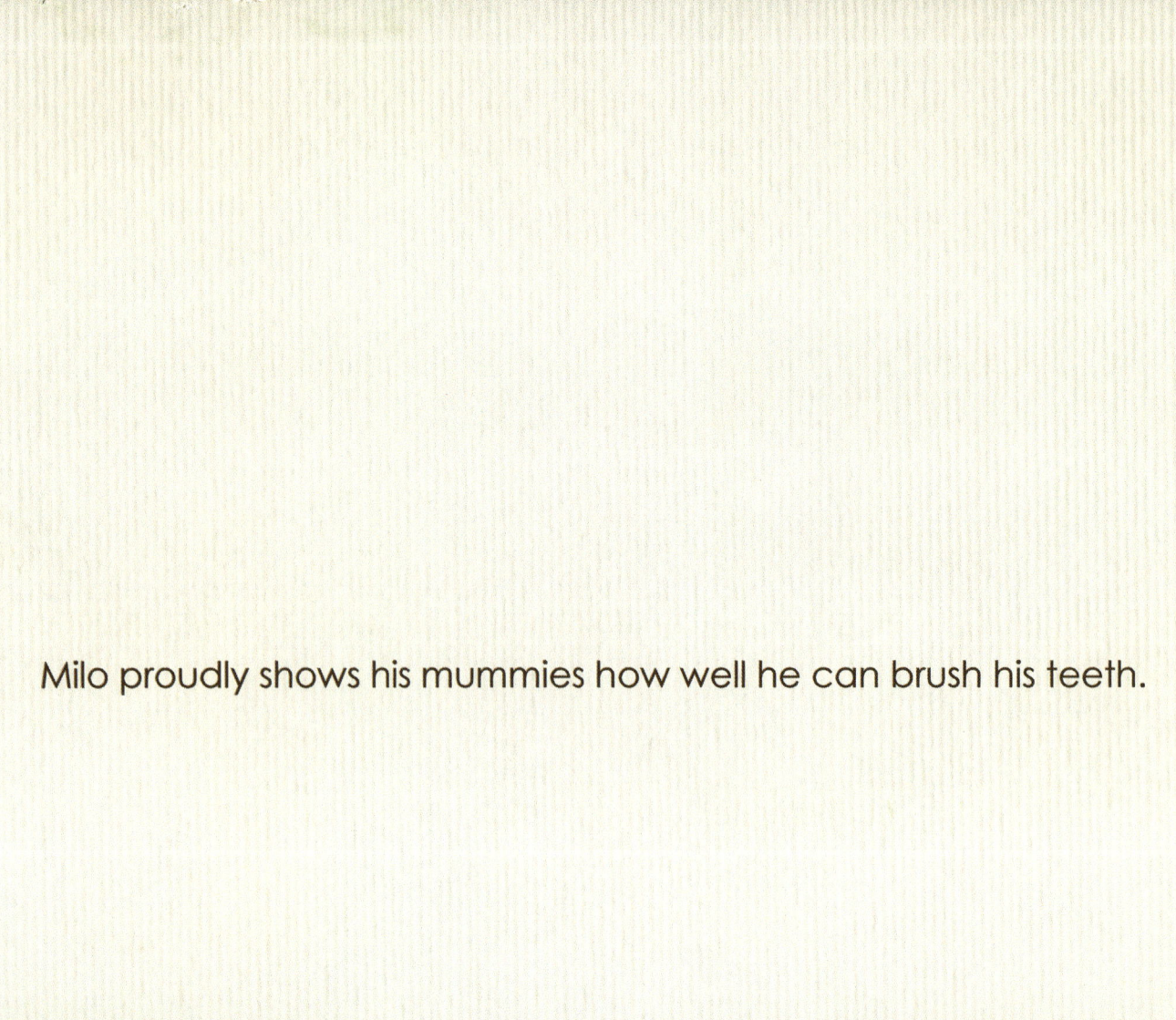

Milo proudly shows his mummies how well he can brush his teeth.

Once Milo is snuggled up into bed Mummy and Mama tell him stories. Milo's favourite stories are the ones where he gets to be the hero in lands filled with dragons and pirates.

Milo also likes hearing the story of when he was born.
Tonight he asks his mummies to tell it to him again.

Milo's Mummies smile, and Mummy answers,
"It all began when Mama and I met and fell in love. We loved
each other very much and decided we would like to start
a family of our own."

"Mummies cannot have babies on their own, so we were introduced to a very nice man who wanted to help us. Together we visited a doctor who helped to make you grow in Mummy's tummy."

"Mummy's belly grew and grew. Mama talked and sang songs to you inside my belly, and gave you lots of kisses."

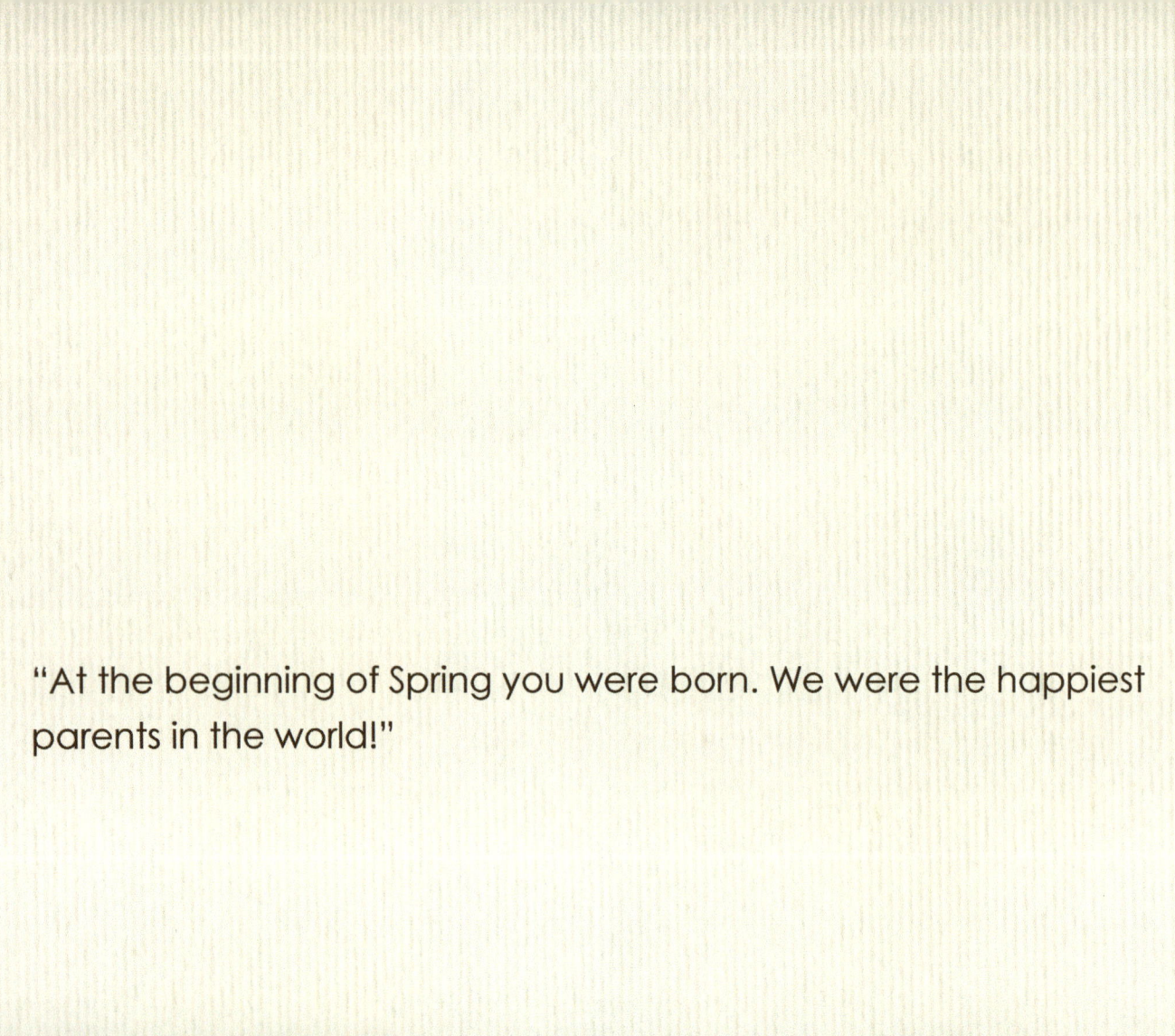

"At the beginning of Spring you were born. We were the happiest parents in the world!"

"You see Milo, families come in many different combinations and that's what makes them special. The important thing is that they love each other.
Some people live with their grandparents...

...some people have one dad,

some people have two dads,

...some people have one mum,

and some people have one mum and one dad."

Milo looks up at his Mummies and smiles.

"I love my two Mummies" he says as Mummy and Mama cuddle
him and gently kiss him goodnight.

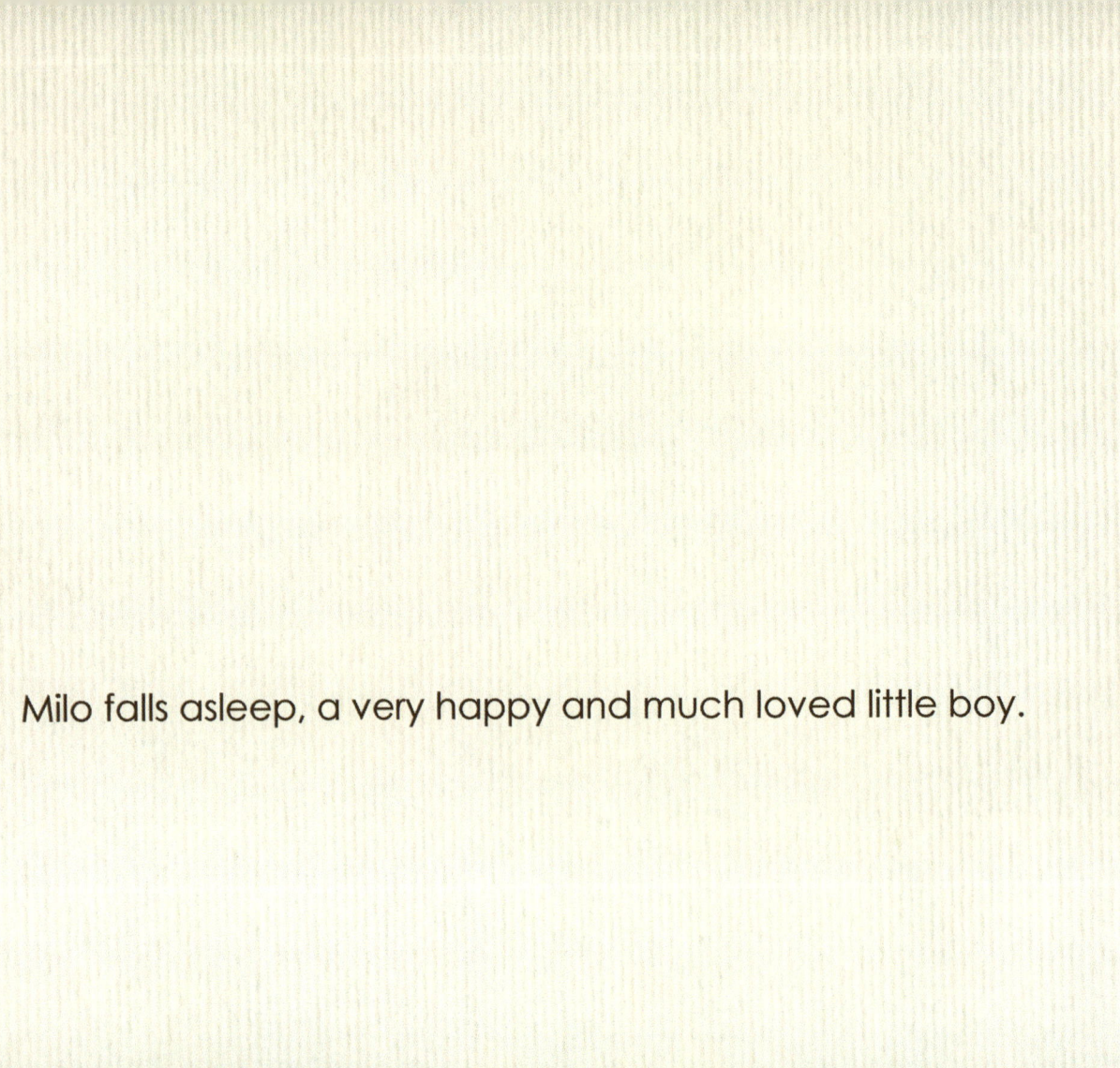

Milo falls asleep, a very happy and much loved little boy.

The end.